DEGREES OF ROMANCE

For
Jill Bialosie
with admiration
Peter

DEGREES OF ROMANCE

PETER KRUMBACH

ELIXIR PRESS
DENVER, COLORADO

DEGREES OF ROMANCE. Copyright © 2024 by Peter Krumbach.
First published by Elixir Press, Denver, Colorado.

Designed by Steven Seighman

Library of Congress Cataloging-in-Publication Data

Names: Krumbach, Peter, author.
Title: Degrees of romance / Peter Krumbach.
Description: First edition. | Denver, Colorado : Elixir Press, 2023. |
Summary: "Winner of the Elixir Press 2022 Antivenom Poetry Award"--
Provided by publisher.
Identifiers: LCCN 2023022344 | ISBN 9781932418828 (paperback)
Subjects: LCGFT: Poetry.
Classification: LCC PS3611.R84925 D44 2023 | DDC 811/.6--dc23/eng/20230721
LC record available at https://lccn.loc.gov/2023022344

ISBN: 978-1-932-41882-8

Library of Congress Cataloging-in-Publication Data TK

First Edition: 2024

10   9   8   7   6   5   4   3   2   1

CONTENTS

II

III

IV

ON *DEGREES OF ROMANCE*

These dazzling prose poems are a portal into "a realm where some great secret is to be divulged, the gate to what's been sought but never found briefly ajar." Enter. Details of ordinary life—the scraping of a spoon, the "fat blue mailbox bolted to a sidewalk"—shimmer like auras the poet reads in the world around us. Part observation, part divination, the poems send messages in invisible ink that appear when you tip them to the sun, the dispatch you've been waiting for.

Degrees of Romance constructs a world from a cool and fevered strangeness, from the collision of language that breaks the boundary between the seen and unseen, from a dense and alluring music—one suspects the poet has found the original divine composition that sang us into being, a song all creatures, the living, the dead, the unborn, are attuned to. A world where even in contradiction we exist in harmony.

One thing transforms into another, kaleidoscopic, a profound act of alchemy animated by animals—grackles, fruit flies, elephants—by humans—grocers, government agents, critics and composers, a flatulent philosopher. They're funny. They pull the unexpected out of a hat shaped like a prose poem that contains multitudes, that travels the space time continuum, so we might "grasp" our "impermanence," "the unweighable bliss of a leaf in an updraft," the day with its "preposterous charm." Like a "pheromoned trail" left by the bellies of ants these poems leave a scent that guides us, fugitives finding our way to each other, to the light that binds us to this world, the lucky ones who mold "confusion into awe."

Candice Reffe, Contest Judge

|

F TRAIN

I followed a nun through the produce section. *I am a Buddhist*, I whispered from behind, *I wish to fit inside a yak's horn*. Her cart was empty. The way she glided in her floor-length tunic suggested she stood on a dolly hauled by a rope. I felt the urge to be that hidden propman, pulling the line, hand over hand, wheeling her around. As hard as I tried, I couldn't glimpse an inch of her flesh, the head deep within the starched coif. There was still a chance the habit was hollow. I rolled a pear under her. She rounded a heap of turnips, then coasted to the eggplants. I began to sweat, hearing voices of Neruda, Ginsberg and Plath, and my nun, my sweet nun, towed through the liquor aisle now, filled her wagon with rye. *Your Reverence? Sister Ann?* The black-and-white headpiece slowly turned and with it the whole store, like a revolving stage scenery sliding off — my nun no longer a nun, but a transit cop tapping my collar with a nightstick, the car full of fluorescence.

A woman on the park bench opens her husband's head. There's another head inside your head, she announces. Well, open it, instructs the husband. The woman reaches in, extracts a rosary, a fungo bat, and then, straining, hauls out the man's mother. To the Mississippi kite, balanced on the tip of the oak's highest branch, this doesn't make sense. It preens its belly, little orgasms rippling the feathers. A slice of its mind signals fulfillment. One eye on the scene below, the other turned inward, the kite pictures lizards and mice regurgitated into the beaks of its young. I told you, Friedrich, shouts the woman as the couple switches positions. Now the man inspects the wife. A column of warm air rises from the meadow. With two strokes of its wings, the kite's adrift in the current. Gliding off, it finds itself soothed by the shriek escaping its throat. From the distance, it hears the husband call out the items pulled from the woman's head — Hypothalamus! Marzipan! Don Giovanni! What's this?

NIGHTSHIFT IN PRODUCE

Big Sal tells me again how he loathes not only the way I stack, but the way I shelve. His words have a rhythm. They become a 5-mile-long train. I nod in triple time, then cut myself adrift, entering a space with no verbs, a field where the past, present and future exist at once. I see my father smoking while eating soup, my mother standing before him in her underwear, holding shears, the kitchen floor Aegean green. I can hear mockingbirds and distant shrieks of children. It is a realm where some great secret is to be divulged, the gate to what's been sought but never found briefly ajar. But then Big Sal points at spinach, and I pray to see what the eye discovers when it shuts, when electricity sends the mind around the track without harness, the jockey asleep in his crib. I need to tell Big Sal that my soul is out back, playing chess against the loading dock crew, that his soul is marked down, bottom shelf, aisle 8. But he's busy, talking about kumquats, and above me, like a giant cotton bloom, a parachute unfurls. I touch down, as I often do, by the pyramid of melons, the spot where someone dropped a brain and stepped in it. The spot Big Sal wants me to orange-cone and mop.

VISITING FUTURE IN-LAWS

For an instant I felt like a portraitist in a ruined coat, summoned to a castle, the Black Forest moon on the horse's tail, the coach tumbling over roots. Right from the start I drank too much, my hands irrational, pouring and lifting, then pouring again. If memory serves me, your parents raised the subject of faith. That's when I said I felt like Pope Innocent X on his throne, baring his fangs, barking from his dark century in Francis Bacon's plum-blue smears. You started to cough, so I said I felt more like Diego Velazquez, putting the last brushstroke on his *Dwarf with a Dog*. Forgive me, Sarah.

EXPLAINING MARRIAGE TO AN ALIEN

No abduction. Just a hoop of light I felt like stepping into. At a folding desk with a box of pens and gum, it sat attempting to look terrestrial. The beard suggested friendliness, each finger sporting a painted nail. The voice? There was no voice. Questions slipped into my head by a wave of its hand. *We know how to swallow the sun, bend time, outrun starlight, we've heard of your wars, greed, and lust. But tell us about marriage.* Marriage? *The bond, the bands, the terms 'husband' and 'wife.' The eight billion of you agree on nothing but marriage.* We must do it. *Whom does it please?* Cake makers at first, then lawyers and priests. *Does it cause happiness?* Yes, a great joy. A heat that grows homicidal. *Don't most of you divorce?* We do. *And those who don't?* They've thought of it. *So, you marry why?* Love. The hand of hundred fingers.

FUGITIVE

We lost a baby. It crowned in the small hours of Monday, I cut the cord at 3:47, and it was gone. The doctor claimed it ran that way, the nurses insisted it fled the other. I rushed the halls, hollered at janitors, the purple-haired lady at the front desk. No matching accounts, only the squeal of tires from the underground garage. Back in your room we shook out the sheets, searched under the gurney, the good nurse combing the trays and troughs, the bad nurse smoking in the bathroom. Should we have foreseen this when the baby was still in? You did mention the baby not kicking but running brisk uterus laps. Could we have studied the sonogram closer, noticed a tiny map in the dot-like fingers? You know what? you said, I wish the baby luck. But what about the crib? I said, All the diapers we bought at Costco? A month later a postcard from Pamplona - the baby running with the bulls. The month after that a selfie with pope Francis in the Vatican Gardens, both wearing miters. And yesterday, a note from Simon & Schuster — the baby's memoir launch. I look at you, you look at your mother, your mother looks at me.

MUSHROOMING

Was it the orange moon that made us crave this flowering, these metabolic wizards thrusting up through moss and bark, flashing their flawless necks like the long-dead roused from their slumber? In the yellow light of our kitchen, we spread them on the checkered cloth and, with what approached triumph, lowered our faces to theirs. We thought we had picked chanterelles. You said everything was edible. Thank you. Now the world is cubist — my hands indiscernible, your hips where your breasts used to be. It appears someone has canceled time so we could reach out to the divine. If this is dying, then let's not rush. Let us hail something animal-drawn and slow, drop into Chekhov's winter — a horse, sleigh, birch grove full of snow. A one-act play with only a table, two chairs and a spotlight. No words, only us, spooning this soup.

CARAVAN

I admire you, toddler caught in my headlights at 2:27 AM, crawling north on all fours in the fast lane of Interstate 5. I know you want me to think I'm dreaming you, so quaint in your naïveté and sequined diaper. I guarantee, toddler, you'll be a judge. Every toe and dimple part of the justice, and as I follow you in first gear — making sure some eighteen-wheeler on meth doesn't swipe you off the road — I pray for you, for your invisible sheep, ducks, and the world's tunnel you gaze into with your huge doubloon eyes. Your body will catch up to your head, toddler, don't worry. Keep crawling, I see no blood. You float, frictionless, an inch above ground. By dawn you'll disappear again, hide somewhere midair, known only to swallows and gnats. I'd love to buy you socks, gloves and kneepads, toddler, or a tiny rolling bed. But you favor unhindered crawl, the breeze kneading your dough. Do you have a breast or two to feed you? At some point you'll need a haircut. Do you mind if I stop my car, give you a sponge bath? You can keep moving while I scrub your back. You look like a cub, toddler. No, you look like the future coming on, passing signs and billboards, ignored by guards and minutemen. Here's my exit, toddler. Can I let you re-enter the unlit night?

WHATEVER IT WAS

Drowsy, still dazed by nightmares, we shuffled to our meditation pads at the bay window. We looked out, and there, on the dead front-yard lawn, among the ceramic gnomes and cinderblocks, it stood. We wobbled into the sharp light and studied its white rhinestoned cape, the moussed hair so black it shone blue. It was life-sized, diaphanous, sunglasses glued onto its swollen face. You reached under its arm and walked it in, all the way to the unused highchair your mother had bought us before your miscarriage. I laid out two bacon strips on a plate before it, just to see what happens. You ate your waffles, I had my corn flakes in 2% milk with a splash of bourbon. The kitchen was quiet, just clicks of spoons on china and tocks of the Ikea clock. We chewed and watched ants advance over the white jumpsuit toward the plate. You had the idea to put on some music. We'd collected vintage vinyl from the seventies, so you put on Never Mind the Bollocks Here's the Sex Pistols and cranked it up. The kitchen slowly filled with anarchy. You tossed it to me and I tossed it back. A grin passed across its face. This must have been the beginning of the end of our grief. The three of us spilled to the backyard and rolled in the grass. By five, drained and hoarse from shrieking, we stood up and watched it pee in the bushes — a lingering act whose image became thinner and thinner, until it merged with the leaves.

HERE

Here is where things we do not know exist
exist. A pneumatic mule, for instance, that
counts the steps of men. A shawl weaved from
universe's nerves. The riding crop of God. His
gun. His boots. A span which makes things we
sense but deem invisible visible. The urge to
procreate, the lure of luster, the compassion-
spite pendulum. Where is the root. How is it
defined (does its definition require definition).
What to do with what it does. How do deeds
done and not done square. And what are the
odds all thoughts ever thought and understood,
have been understood incorrectly. Who is
asking these questions and does anyone care.
Good morning.

TUESDAY

I eat pudding. The fighter jet, thousands of feet above me, barrel rolls, the pilot's horizon spinning like a Dutch mill. I hear the distant roar, scrape the plastic cup with a spoon. It's Tuesday. I like to drive slow, past the parking lot's dying hedges, the fat blue mailbox bolted to the sidewalk. It pleases me. Day, after day, after day, it is there. Today, beside that box, orange-robed and sandaled, stands a Buddhist monk. He is still, shaved skull bent down, looking at his phone. I head to the library. A monthly meeting of poets and anti-poets in a cell-sized room. When I arrive, they already speak of burials. By now the jet pilot might have slipped out of her mirror-vizored helmet and walked toward a canteen where someone waits. The 84-year-old woman across the table from me describes a couple who has chosen to be buried in coffins stacked on top of each other in one grave. All of us nod and reach for grapes laid out in a small wire basket shaped like a pig. The library walls are thin. I can hear the group in the next room. They discuss 3D-printed guns. Someone laughs so hard he begins to cough, then gag. I remind myself it is still Tuesday. What's the pilot up to now? Having sex with her wife, or husband? Or her weapon's officer, whose ex-fiancé's at the funeral of an aunt who happened to be a co-worker of the man whom I'm watching through the window cross Draper Street, almost being hit by a silver Lexus? We read poems, and the pale-green grapes are seedy and warm. Thank you, I say to Estelle, who brought them and sits to my right. What? she says. The people behind the wall have now switched to prostates or preserves, it's not very clear, since they've lowered their voices. Laura is reading her poem about a family violin, a lovely piece that ends with the word, "Jakarta." I'm giving her my compliments and as I pause to search for the correct praise, the two wings of the swing door open. A frail, elderly woman in a motorized wheelchair backs into the room. A young caretaker runs after her from the hall, stops the chair, and apologizes. Two poets rise to hold the wings open and the caretaker wheels the woman back out into the hall. Now I don't remember the gist of my compliment. On the way home, stuck in traffic, I have almost completely forgotten the jet pilot and her lover, and think of the wheelchair lady, the way she turned her head and seemed to have peeked at me before they took her away. And I think of Sharon, telling us that in New Orleans cemeteries, when you stop paying rent, they evict the bodies.

MEDITATION WITH A WRONG TURN

A newborn has 300 bones. 300 blocks that one by one disappear — poof — poof — poof — until there are just 206 to haul for the rest of one's life. Does nature want to continue? Do strings? Do quarks? Knock knock. Who's there? A body in a chair, loading and emptying its lungs, enlivening the blood. The I's urge to escape one's skin—to return into the open, trying to forgive itself for inviting fear, for tying simplicity into complicated knots. Ah, the body's prison — hot, unthinking, lovingly stupid, heeding some primordial command to build and tear down. How to separate judgment from discernment, flatten inner life into painted wood — an altar triptych without Christ. How to ignore the medieval lord, suddenly there, holding a pheasant thigh, belching, requesting mutton — an ancient feast about to erupt. How to forgive oneself for thinking about thinking, for neglecting the heart, for making a wrong turn in the spacetime continuum, for acknowledging the clatter of silver, bloodhound yelps, the drone of a lute, for beginning to smell of burnt tallow, venison and funk.

HOME INVASION

They must have picked the lock. No scratches Professional. Small footprints in the shag. No mayhem of razored pillows. In fact, the sofa cushions straightened. The action mostly in the kitchen. The fridge, my wife claims, is a safe with no bolt. The gloved hand must have pulled the heavy door, reached into the light, extracted the cool carton of cage-free browns. I picture the flashlight beam, the glass bowl filling with water at the bottom of the sink, one by one the eggs slid in, clinking against the glass. Perhaps no flashlight, instead a brazenly thrown switch, a bold brightness. Before vanishing, they had done our laundry, ironed and folded, the air still scented with soap. The note on the table terse, left-handed, *The eggs float.* In the kitchen, the detective, my wife, me. From the flannel bush beyond the window the banter of two towhees.

LIFE INSURANCE
(FREE CONSULTATION)

Say I'm killed by lightning while feeding a horse. A light drizzle, the meadow wide and lush. Say the horse is cinnamon-brown with steam rising off its hide. The animal's lips lovingly warm, sugar cubes in my palm. Will the happiness survive? *If any part of you survives, the negotiated benefit cannot be released and will be retained by the custodian bank until you've fully expired.* Were I to haunt my house, make my spouse sense a sudden chill as I bow to kiss her neck, have the wine in her glass ripple enough to catch her eye and make her shudder, would I be considered dead? *Technically speaking, yes — provided you had been successfully cremated or interred.* Is it possible the death of all my memories causes a vortex that violates my past, including this contract? *No. Sixty days after your exit, the stipulated sum is transferred to the designated beneficiary.* Can I sign with my blood — the lone authentic ink, the carrier of stardust whose crimson may not be crimson at all? *We use DocuSign, for discreet digital processing and safekeeping. Any other questions?* Dying seems so crude. Can't I just disappear? *That might be a problem. Without a death certificate, the policy won't be executed.* What if *I'm* executed. *As long as we have evidence — preferably video footage — then everything's fine.*

THE DUCK

It was the moment when all eight of us suffered the same seizure, the one that marks each dinner party, the instant of sticky silence when you pretend to eat the duck, trawling your halted mind for a thing to say. It was then that I startled myself proposing that we all undress. I suspected you would be the first to get on board, maybe your sister Lydia, and Stan, her husband, who had spent the evening eyeing Yolanda, whose one reckless breath could have burst her tube top into confetti. Perhaps the blue-cheeked man brooding to my left like an unfinished statue of Richard Nixon. But no — it was old Professor Lustig who stood up at the head of the table, and, in the gleam of his wife's cutlery, began to loosen his tie.

MIDWAY

—for R. S.

Ron says in a lifetime we each swallow fourteen spiders. That's about a spider every five years, I say. It's 92 degrees. We stand on the sidewalk between Luna's Psychic Reading and Happy Head (Foot Reflexology and Massage). Ron has been married four times, almost killed twice. The last few weeks he's been contemplating building a canoe. To remind myself, he says, what birch-bark and cedar ribs can do for the spirit. What do you know about chickens, I say. I raised chickens in 1954, he says, bought a rooster from Sears & Roebuck, the hens I got from one-armed Frank who had fifteen and ran out of space. I ask him about the ants in my kitchen, storming from everywhere like columns of Mongolian horse-archers. Almost blind, says Ron, inhaling for a long sentence about pheromoned bellies with which they mark their trails. The bus is late. A gray-haired man with a deep tan ambles toward us. Pushes a stroller. The small cardboard sign fastened to its canopy says Mademoiselle Michelle. Beneath it sits a black-and-white dog of an uncertain lineage, frail and old, the bottom of the rig stuffed with tightly twined bundles. The fellow passes with a wide toothless grin. Ron grins back. I study the dog, the man stops for me to get a better look. I can't remember the last time I wept, but right there something sticks to me like a leech to a host. My fingers feel the warm neck of the animal. As I raise my head to talk, Ron begins waving at the approaching bus as if he knew the driver, or maybe to test if we're visible.

THE DRIP

Hanging off the hose bib lip, this bead
has translated into an all-side mirror.
It holds the sky, the tree to my right,
this sun-drenched wall, the ant on the
flagstone, this me, crouched, leaning in.
It shows what I am to water—no different
than rocks and dirt or the Canada
geese rowing overhead. A man on one
knee, bent over a drip, considering
impermanence, aquifers and moisture
of interstellar clouds. How delicious
this second. And now another, a new me
in it.

ODE TO KO

Wow!

Thank you for this uneven darkness. From nowhere a left cross and now the tilt, the transition to quarter speed, the floating spit orbiting the mouthguard. How lovely to find all things asleep. Praise the swoon's permission to embrace gaps, become a mole burrowing through earth. Praise the night travel between the skull's east and west, the flight across black surf strewn with plankton light. Praise that fraction of an inch the mind shifts to oblige the blow.

HYDROGEN AND HELIUM

I misspell people's faces. Cup them in my palms, kiss some, give a playful tug on the jowls of others. *Good evening. Never better.* Burghers of landfills and oak-lined boardrooms, white-collar criminals and donors of kidneys. Calculated together, they equal a mean designed to obscure the edges. *I apologize, parties do this to me.* The low ceiling track lights, the shag underfoot, the heads bobbing like olives in brine. *I could have sworn it was Frank. Dressed as Biff.* I bend to greet the elders collapsed in mid-century chairs. Boredom, meet urgency. I bend to your aunt Wilma, who turns out to be your stepfather's 94-year-old cousin Lou. *Forgive me.* To regard the room is to learn constellations. The ochre in the white of certain eyes. I'm not the only one bending. Notice Larry —or is it Barry — how he bows to smell the toothpick-pierced prosciutto rolls. *Do I need air?* Out on the deck, two PhDs and an Anglican dean lighting a blunt. *Why did the universe start off with hydrogen and helium?* The PhDs chuckle. Way too young for their degrees. The dean holds his breath, then exhales fine haze. *Pardon my bladder.* On the bathroom mirror, someone wrote $N = R \times f_p \times n_e \times f_l \times f_i \times f_c \times L$ in coral rouge. Stepping out, I hear someone suggest a duel by the pool. A reenactment of Pushkin versus d'Anthès. *A thousand dreams that never were.* For you, I play Pushkin. It works. I come to supine, you kneeling in the grass, hand on my head. I point at the leaves. Red, white, red, white, the ambulance strobe-lights salsa with the trees.

TRANSATLANTIC

This alone. The man on the TSA line right in front of you, carrying caribou antlers. Yes, you drank. Yet no doubt. There he stands with the horns. And guess what. He looks like Ted Berrigan. He may be Ted Berrigan. What do you tell Ted Berrigan hauling a set of antlers? Hello Ted? No. You begin to talk about the eleven-foot narwhal tusk the lady ahead of him wheels atop her suitcase. Narwhal, says Ted. Basically a beluga whale. The tusk one of its two teeth. The TSA folks snap their blue rubber gloves against their wrists. The one who reminds you of Anne Waldman, ca 1966, walks over to Ted and asks for his belt. Then your boots. The woman with the tusk is petitioned by three agents to hold her arms out *like a pelican*. You expect to be quizzed. About bear spray and bicycle chains. Whether you saw anyone pack cymbals, darts, or fertilizer into your luggage. Do you journey with fire extinguishers, throwing stars, snow globes, or sand? But no one wants to know. Even the president on the overhead TV is indifferent, the other screen stressing the shortage of corn, the wisdom of gold. And Ted is being patted, the antlers a Joshua tree high above his hair. You calculate the distance to the gate where the burnished dildo of the plane rests on its gear. And what does Anne do? She waves you through, putting makeup on empty space, painting the phenomenal world. Her palms cup your heart. A tiny joy, then another. You will be late.

THE LAST FERRY

—for L.D.

I talk to a Portuguese fisherman. It turns out he's a fisherman but not Portuguese. He is Basque. We speak Portuguese. To be exact, I speak Portuguese and he replies in Basque which I do not understand. A Portuguese fisherman stands beside us, translating from Basque to Portuguese, periodically from Basque to English, then to Portuguese and back to Basque. I ask about fish. Learn that the Basque is actually not a fisherman. He rents fishermen — most of whom are Portuguese (some Basque) — his boats. They pay him in fish or Portuguese promissory notes (occasionally Basque coins). The Basque man knows little about fish. It is becoming apparent to me that I should have spoken only to the Portuguese fisherman who is translating, as opposed to the Basque man who is not only a non-fisherman but does not speak any of the languages I do. This has taken about fifteen minutes. The tide is beginning to come in. People in the motel spoke all day about the approaching storm. First drops hit the Portuguese fisherman's face. The Basque boat owner rests his eyes on the dark-gray sea. There's a strong smell of fish in the air.

EARL

We sat on stools and discussed which one of us would expire first, and whether Earl was the man to preserve us. It was unclear if this was his hobby or profession. We'd thought he only taxidermized celebrities' pets. But then we saw him crossing the yard carrying Mickey Rooney. We'd already had a stuffed owl from your father's estate, looking nice on the dresser. But a wool-filled spouse? Having to dust it, polish the glass eyes, cleaning cobwebs from between the legs? Still, we rang Earl's bell to ask about his rates. He answered the door, a deer under his arm, the animal's chest slit, trickling what looked like hay onto the floor. You opened with Is that hay? No, said Earl, that's woodwool. We walked down the hallway into a cluttered den. Earl leaned the deer against the wall and watched us settle on the couch. Earl, I said, would you be willing to stuff one of us? Earl's fingers slid through his hair. I'm fully booked right now, he said, lowering himself on a chair. When were you thinking? We don't know yet, you said, just wondering about the cost. Depends, said Earl, for neighbors, I'd probably knock some off. Can you give us a ballpark? I said. Earl exhaled, trilling his lips. A thousand for her, seven-fifty for you? he said. Makes sense, I said. You turned to me, but I kept looking at Earl and the deer behind him. What do you mean *Makes sense?* you said. Earl leaned back. Let me put it this way, Janet, he said. You have more surface. When we got home, I put on Jeopardy and you shut it off. I cooked spaghetti and we ate in silence. By the smell coming from the yard, we could tell the nuns on the other side of the cyclone fence were again grilling with gasoline. I went to the sink and turned on the water. It sounded like TV static, the whoosh swallowing everything in the room. I felt you sidling up to my right. I washed the dishes and you dried.

FOR MY WIFE'S SECOND COUSIN WHO CAME TO VISIT FOR A WEEK AND STILL SLEEPS IN OUR GUESTROOM

Perhaps it's time, Randall, to move on, re-enter the Smoky Mountains with their elk and your distillery business. It's been a vivid year for us — two house fires, a police raid, your Christmas hospitalization. Thank you. Not only for the bongs and fuzzy slippers, but the endless stories of Dark Web and Anglo-Saxon lore. You are dear to us, Randall, please wake up. Linda has emptied your ashtrays, I snaked the toilet again. It flushes now, you can stop using the sink, except for washing. God bless. The towels are meant for drying your skin, as opposed to blotting blood off the floor. Understand, Randall, we could drive you to the depot, would be glad to secure a one-way ticket to Huntsville where your brother runs a chain of gentlemen's clubs. No, thank *you*. We had a ball. Linda and I adore you. Is that a hookah pipe? Okay. Tomorrow then? We'll help you pack. Pardon? I guess we have some cash. How much were you thinking? Didn't we spot you 500 last week? You need a thousand? *Plus* the ticket?

II

HERE IS THE BODY

Here is the body's one-room shack
cranked slowly up the rails to the top
of the coaster. Here is the body's fog
swaddling the glow of its maraschino
heart. Here is the body courting the mind.
Here is the body propagating. Here is
the body pulled toward a distant star
whose gravity feels sweeter. Here is
the body on ten-foot stilts determined
to win a hundred-yard dash. Here is
the body divorcing the mind. Here is
the body's itch to divorce itself. Here is
the body filled with wilted geraniums.
Here is the body letting a bumblebee
circle its pinkish dark. Here is the body
laughing, its windows and doors ajar.

ON PUZZLEMENT

In the '50s, a CIA man designed a jail-break kit that could be contained in a rectal suppository. He conceived tie-clip spy cameras and ultra-thin needles to inject poisons into sealed bottles of wine. He tested mind-altering blends, sometimes in fatal doses, on unsuspecting prisoners and brothel johns. Every day he'd return to his plumbing-free cabin where he lived with his wife. All along, he studied Buddhism, meditated, grew vegetables, got up before the roosters to milk his goats. After retiring, he moved to India to volunteer in leprosariums. When I was three, I wondered whether I'd sprouted from the ground like a head of lettuce. It is the first thought I can remember, my first stride toward bewilderment. Today I saw a white shirt kiting high above the city, aimless like a ghost of a swan. Maybe we are meant to die of confusion once it peaks and turns to awe.

SUBJECT X

The goggles made everything look upside down and showed the left as the right and the right as left. He was told to get up and walk. He fell over. The plan was to have him wear the specs day and night for a month. Soon, he not only strode around his house and the neighborhood without falls, he also rode a bicycle through the Mission District, sailed a sloop and was able to fly kites. He had struggled with dyslexia, bafflement and phobias, was nonverbal, colorblind, and claimed not to hear. Distrusting the alphabet, he'd sign his name by drawing a square with an umlaut. At the end of the trial, when they removed his glasses, not only did he begin to speak, but all his past ailments were gone, he was 1.4 inches taller, gained 6 pounds of muscle, and could fence. However, though born in San Jose, he was now speaking Flemish, and - with the help of an interpreter – insisted he was still allergic to cats. When asked whether he'd be willing to donate his brain to the Agency, he replied, Hoe zit het met mijn ballen? This experiment became later known as The Fleming.

ON PUBLISHING

You outline a novel about a man who eats angels. A man who, in the mist of spitting oil, jerks the handle of a wok. A decent man with a flaw. After a meal of ribs, your publisher ponders how certain cuts of veal remind him of tiny calves, how far he's willing to trust your relationship with devotion. Hours slip by. At 3 a.m. he calls your agent. Your agent picks up on the second ring. No, he answers, it's a fictional account. The line goes quiet. The publisher drinks warm milk. It helps him sleep. In the morning your agent calls to tell you about his dream. You listen and nod, saying nothing, because your chair faces the publisher who's observing you from behind his desk. His magnified, swimming eyes watch your every move, the way you switch the phone right ear to left. Is this the end of beauty? he asks when you hang up. Hot gusts rustle the palm fronds outside the open window, bring the smell of Santa Ana sand. You show him a coin. Look, you say and flick it high in the air. The instant is brief. Both of you wedged between the future and the past, gazing up, watching it flip end over end, beginning over beginning, each rotation a tiny glint — end, beginning, end, beginning, end, beginning, end.

BANK JOB

What am I doing on a train to Philadelphia? Chewing bills someone on the platform gave me as change for a hundred, and when I take them out of my mouth, they are frayed and Canadian. So I wake up. It's 10! Quick—bathroom, face in water, must call office, make up a story. Who will pick up the phone? The churl from Loans? Pregnant Tara? Larry? Then I wake up, *really* wake up, unemployed, yet still somehow late for something. I plunge my head under the cold faucet, make sure this *is* being awake. What time is it? My body keeps waltzing, oblivious to temporal constraints. It doesn't think of death, only I do, but I'm not the body, I'm the 21 grams that leave when the dancing stops. And I wake up again, this time for real, because the subway smell is real, and Aida, the bank guard, holds the door for me and says Good morning. It must be real because for an instant I see a tiger tackling the teller, dragging the limp body by the neck toward the vault. Then everything quiets again. The day is ready for its preposterous charm, the magnolia blooms bobbing behind the pane. How can I help you?

HARMONY

It was a Sunday that felt as if the universe decided to restring its harps. The blue-black grackles brought their own shadows to walk on, and realtors exposed their well-meaning teeth. There was the movement of bare shoulders and the gurgle of poured wine. Two short dogs, drunken on birdsong, sniffed each other beneath the oak's low bow. There were no bad intentions—goodness so thick, the Devil joined a game of bocce. The river kept to its business of carving the dale, passing the poplars where, circled by preschoolers in bright hats, sat an enormous tin tub. And right there, among the shrieks of bliss, in his navy-blue suit, knelt the President, bobbing for apples. A little girl pointed at the corpse submerged underneath the floating fruit. The President held a Braeburn in his mouth, the front of his coiffure drenched flat, wet strands covering his eyes. *Yes,* a beaming security agent whispered to the girl, bending closer to her ear, *someone has drowned. And let me tell you something else young lady — just before people die, they brighten.* And the moment he said that, there came helicopters with their own remarkable wind and rotating heat, and against the sky the propellers whipped in triangular smudges. And everything, everything reflected in the river. And surely the fish were listening. The pebbles and the mud were listening. The small porcupine, the grass, the scree, the swallows swooping into midge clouds with open beaks, all listening.

GOD WATCHING A
SLEEPING MAN

He breathes through his nose, his mouth, then the entire twenty-two square feet of his skin. I let his eyes roll, dream of the underground. I show him worms and quartz, turn him into a big-headed mole rat, make him see with his snout. His body-smell, caught in a draft, slips out the open window, into oak leaves. I can end his life, let his tongue drop into his throat, have him see white. White so white it turns black and tight, like patience trapped in rocks. But I let him live, let him snore, wake with dry mouth, paw the dark. Watching him, I ponder the degree to which he's me. After raving on Fridays, when he collapses into linen, I have him walk in his sleep. Yes, it is cruel. I am cruel. And kind. But mostly cruel. I let him trip, stray naked into the neighbors' yard, ram their grill with his erection, cannonball into their spa. I tug on strings to pull him out, to sway his arms, curl his lip. He may be rich, with jelly-slicked hair, but when he sleeps, he's like everyone else. Why kill him when I can sow doubt, hide his rings, roll a grape to the toe of his shoe?

11:37

She steps out of the bathroom dressed only in cards. Their values facing out, he can, even in the lowered light of her bedroom, clearly spot the pips, the swaying jacks, the ten of diamonds that her thighs turn side to side as she struts along the bed. A fresh deck, can you smell? She reaches for him with one hand, the other holding a glass with two jokers drowned in gin. The window is open to the late-August heat. The pigeon on the sill bobs, then glides toward the tail-light lava eight floors below. It lands on the sidewalk, instantly drunk on the scent of burnt pistachios strewn by the feet of two laughing hustlers. One of them will, later that night, maim a man and not remember. The stoplight above them is alive, memorizing the miens of cabbies and cops, the drifting moods of ambulance howls. Beneath the awning glints a small blue stone in the lobe of a bicycle thief talking on his phone. Across the street the card man's wife leans against her car and smokes, her eyes trained on the high open window, its yellow so faint now, it is possible that what she sees isn't happening.

SECOND DATE

From the next table a toddler boy in a high chair torques his torso one-hundred-and-eighty degrees to face me. On his chest a green rubber bib, its bottom edge curled up to form an inch-deep trough. The woman I am with speaks of dolphins. I think of objects to feed the wobbly cherub, his immense black irises fixed on my bald head. I palm a cheese cracker the way a city hall clerk would a cash-laden envelope. My date is a surfer. I am finding out that her niece has constructed a toy guillotine. The boy grasps the cracker, then drops it on the floor, his eyes never leaving my head. Downward dog. My companion teaches yoga. I have a dachshund, I say. The almond of my hypothalamus is beginning to glow, approaching the liberty of ruin, the strength-gathering conviction I can now say anything I want without the burden of subsequent proof. I'm the youngest of fourteen children, my parents are miners, I graduated from Stanford, play viola and volunteer as a security guard at the farmers market. She orders another glass of Chablis. The high-chair boy turns to me again, a lit battery-powered candle now inserted in his mouth, his cheeks illuminated from within. They blaze pink. It is so beautiful I want to weep. Yes, I've heard of hot yoga, I hear myself answer.

GAMEKEEPER'S NIGHTS

Lately I sleepwalk through several doors until I reach a one-acre field with a one-room house. A man named Carl lives there. He turns up the earth with an ox and a plow. I watch him from the bushes, realizing after a while that he is me, Carl is me, and this plot of land, the small house, the ox and the geese flying soundlessly, are all inside my head. This goes on for a while as I sleep. It turns out, I don't sleepwalk, just lie in my bed under a thin blanket in a slightly bigger house, a cabin really, that is not in the middle of a field, but in the middle of a forest. And, of course, I am someone else's dream, as he watches from the bushes, sees me wake up and go about my business of walking from tree to tree, putting nametags on the bark, feeding the magpies that land on the brim of my hat. Then the man in the bushes realizes he is me, and the cycle continues. I suspect this has been going on for quite some time.

THE WORD PROBLEM EFFECT

When a raindrop begins to descend from the height of one mile over York, Pennsylvania, it is four o'clock in the afternoon. The drop is gray blue, partially magenta. At the same time in Lexington, Kentucky, train A leaves the station heading west. In its dining car, seated at a small square table by the first window, proctologist Edwin Potts observes his napkin. It is seven o'clock in Coeur D'Alene, Idaho, when at the altitude of two miles a snowflake is formed. Seventeen-hundred-and-eight structure beams comprise its white filigree. The wind is steady from north east at twelve-point-six knots. Directly below it, four buses (B, C, D & F) depart in various directions. One carries passengers, the remaining three stacked with mannequins. Their destinations lie at thirty-degree increments from one another, starting with due north, continuing counter-clockwise (when perceived from the vantage of the flake). The engineer of the Kentucky train (A), Ricardo Goldscheib, (blood type A+), has just applied ten milligrams of Preparation H to his itch. If two white goats, communicating with each other through a series of pelvic nudges and bleats, walk along Interstate 110, heading towards San Pedro, California, the female being two inches taller than the male, and Cindy Lauper (no relation to the singer) drives her Toyota Corolla in the opposite direction while texting her beau (blood type AB-) in La Junta, Colorado, what is, on a scale from 0 to 7, the chance of all the above to affect the flight of a single purple martin, age 4?

THE LESSON

—for A.S. and M.S.

Don't get me wrong. I love evening strolls. Avery, my petite 93-year-old philosopher neighbor, his wife Mildred, and me. Stepping slowly. Down the darkening walk. Avery repeatedly asking how I'm doing. Mildred, a 91-year-old medieval historian, narrating exhaustively, speaking with precision. "In fact," the recurring phrase. I mention the logic of providence. Avery, chortling, brings up David Hume. He ambles between Mildred and me, and as he muses on Hume's problem of induction, he begins to pass wind. The volume is remarkable. I look at Mildred. Not a hint of acknowledgement. Does she think it's me and is being polite? She can't be hard of hearing; it's always been Avery asking "Come again?" Does she know it is him and no longer flinches? He keeps walking, shifting to Frege's theory of sense and denotation. As he does, another round of flatulence. I'm trying to focus on what he's stating. As we stop for a moment, his farting escalates to such an alarming pitch, I'm beginning to fear the worst. Mildred grows quiet, her eyes pointed straight up at the emerging stars of Seven Sisters. Avery restarts his stroll, switching to Wittgenstein. Now the flatulence is almost constant, as if encouraged by his speech. I can't hear half of his words. Mildred keeps studying the sky, her silence adding more prominence to the blasts. I can no longer follow, able to merely offer "yes" or "I see," glancing sideways at Avery's pants. He talks of Karl Marx now, I think. We're on our way back, approaching my house. A woman striding in the opposite direction passes and glares at me through the noise. We reach my front door. I bid them good evening and fumble with keys. From the threshold I watch the slow vanishing, their hands joined now, the gray heads like two moths entering a mine.

TELEGRAM FROM THE NEW WORLD

ONLY FIVE DEATHS - JOURNEY CALM - GOD KIND - BRIEF
GOAT STAMPEDE IN AFT HOLD - DOCTOR TIPSY - UNCLE
BOR INJURED - MILD HUMPED MAN FROM SICILY GIFTS
OLIVES - MANY SMELLS AND CARD GAMES - POLISH
CHILD PECKED BY PELICAN - SHORTAGE OF LIMES -
BEFRIENDED CAPTAIN -   SHOWED ME HIS GLASS EYE
- SUGGESTED MARRIAGE - MOST POTATOES ROTTEN -
WORMS IN OATS - SKY FOUR TIMES HIGHER THAN BACK
HOME - LADIES IN BLACK - DULCIMERS - PRIEST IN
CROW'S NEST - BOHEMIANS POINTING AT WHALES -
NEW WORDS - DREAM OF PASSENGER'S HAT - RUSSIAN
COBBLER CAUGHT FEEDING RATS - FIGHT WITH FIRST
OFFICER - TWELVE DAYS NO STORM - NEW WORLD
HARBOR - CARRIAGES ON QUAY - LARGE MEN
STAMPING MANIFESTS - I MUST SIGN - NEW NAME -
NEW NAME - NEW NAME - THREE TIMES - BREAD WITH
ONIONS - DOGS AND HORSES TALLER THAN BACK HOME
- HOUSES OF STEEL - BEAUTIFUL DIN - COPPER COINS -
SOOT - WIDE STREETS LINED WITH DUNG - RAPID
CARTS - FEVER - BUY FIRST MEAL - CABBAGE AND SPUDS -
THINK OF YOU BEFORE SLEEP - WILL YOU COME - THIS
IS MY NEW NAME - ELIZABETH

FOXWHELP

I ordered a Foxwhelp. I meant no offense. No reason for the maître d'
to slide so quickly to our table and hiss like a straight razor on a cheek.
My calves lost sensation, and everyone was sizing my lips. So, again,
I said *I'll have a Foxwhelp*. When the clenched-jaw owner arrived, I
watched your father unbutton his frock, and your stepmother's
fingertips find her temples. Two busboys began rolling up the carpet
next to us and somehow I noticed the foreigners at the corner booth
holding high above their heads a long iridescent fish. I turned to you,
but your eyes studied the ceiling frescos. When the chef's banana-
fingers landed by my plate, the numbness had spread from the calves
all the way to my groin. I am a decent man, I thought, a man who reads
four papers, shampoos your pussy, and grooms your pugs. A man
whose transgressions had long been expunged, all his chickens
hatched. So why the sirens? Why the cuffs and the buzzcut cop
palming my skull, folding me into the cage of his cruiser?

THE PROBLEM WITH TRUTH

Inside the golden-yellow sheen of anger that drapes over chairs, lamps, and the gnomes outside the window, I listen to my wife and foot by foot enter the house of void. I feel the way a forgotten stadium in the middle of a jungle does, vines wrapping the pungent mist into irregular lumps. I advance through the hall. No furniture anywhere, only the scent of coconut monkeys who have chosen the bedroom closet to sleep with their toy pebbles. My wife is repeating something and I nod, yet I am standing alone, shoes in a slight V below my briefcase, hanging from my shoulders a suit jacket, but the pants and underwear are gone, freeing my south to the breeze from the west. *I know*, I say. The twins we don't yet have are asleep, matching pajamas, plastic rifles, the dummy's head chewed off by the dog. But this is not true. I do not have a wife, the children have beards and are older than me, which would mean I'm closing in on something. This is what happens at board meetings each Monday, Larry stands and points at the white board, and shit begins to fly.

RUMORVILLE

Mathematicians don't have friends. Astrophysicists: kinky. Oceanographers: beige, stringy, often unaware of holes in their hearts. Chronologists will not shut up. Chemists: introverted onanists who wear a single suit their entire life. Geologists smoke one pipe before breakfast. Archeologists: their egos require separate passports. Meteorologists: carnivores (some prizing flesh of hapless Botanists). Molecular Biologists will claim their genitals as dependents. Engineers: the worst (too many reasons to list here). Ecologists make babies with Zoologists, then pee on them. Epistemologists make babies with Logicians, breathe only through their nose. The safest? Theoretical Linguists. Most dangerous? Alcoholic Semanticists. Pragmatists: essentially a sadistic strain of Normative Psychologists. Empiricists originated the term *hockey puck*. Sociologists: mild, thin-haired and concupiscent. Geographers: often found feuding with Cartographers. Pathologists: bluebeards living in fear of defenestration. Taxonomists despise being confused with Taxidermists. Immunologists tend to marry Pathologists. Geneticists: very good dancers. Herpetologists: mostly overfed, certain bones transparent. Ornithologists: sensitive, notorious for collecting tears of Criminologists. Ethicists: not for sale, eleven months in hibernation, one month looking for a mate. Economists: basically Statisticians, without the charisma.

PROFESSOR ANGUS

"If you stoop to lame alliteration again, I will cane you in front of the class. If you squeeze out one more villanelle, I swear I'll snap your femurs and feed your nuts to my goats. To chance upon a true line in your lyrical sludge is like spotting an orchid in elephant dung. Your adverbs, interjections, allusions and innuendos line my mule-foot pig's pen. Oh, you want to say something? You've published an essay in The Hanging Chad? *Coordination resulting in poetic rather than analytic attention, implying aesthetic order or resolution rather than an authentic rendering of the ultimately irresolvable shades of logical distinction in a complex reality.* Is that what you'd rather discuss? Not today, not tomorrow, not on the Ides of March. Look at your verse, you lily-livered dips. Where's the urge to slash, to burn? Oh, you think I'm bitter? You bet I'm bitter. I have mouths to feed, a spouse who won't fuck and elders who TV-binge from dawn to dusk. And I just found I'm allergic to walnuts! So don't Petrarchan sonnet me, don's cento me, leave those sestinas gestate in your arse. Look at me, you periwinkles – you've got 15 minutes to write 15 lines. I'll be outside, smoking, inventing reasons not to hurt myself."

III

TCHAIKOVSKY

It was when I scrubbed that hideous yellow rug that I found him under the bed. Surprisingly odorless, considering he had to have lain there for all those years. He was so small. Maybe a shade over five feet, a teal cravat still tied under his chin. *Pyotr Ilyich?* I said, wishing he'd open his eyes and exhale some Saint Petersburg haze. But he just lay there with his brown shoes and hands tucked into his waistcoat. I picked him up and carried him to the kitchen. Why was he so light? Had the bulk of death long been sucked out? I sat him in the chair and tapped on his chest. The tip of his tongue slipped through the beard. I ran to the bathroom to fetch a brush. I wanted to comb his hair before taking him to the station. But when I returned, he was under the table, face down in a puddle of milk. Still no pulse. I mopped, then remembered the thick roll of butcher paper and twine in the pantry. Wrapping the head first, I swaddled him down all the way to his feet. We got on the trolley at Prudhomme and Main. The conductor charged me extra *for the swordfish* under my arm. By the time we got to the station, he'd become heavier. I leaned him against the wall outside the restroom. It felt good to splash cold water on my neck, then on the mirror, study my warped reflection in the droplets gliding slowly toward the center of the Earth. I listened for their music, but only heard the soft ringing in my ears. When I stepped out, he was gone. I circled the hall for a while, lighting a cigarette, peeking under benches, then bought two tickets to Trenton and headed for the Lost-and-Found. The clerk dipped beneath the counter and produced an umbrella, a set of dentures, and four unclaimed hats. I could hear the train pulling into the station. The announcer coughed over the loudspeakers and as I ran, it felt as though the deceased and the unborn were watching me from afar. I could almost see them, in black and white, the distance taking away their faces. Out on the platform, the cars stood quiet, sooted, the windows redirecting light. I thought about the restroom mirror, how it was wide enough to leap through, if I were that kind of a man.

POLICE INTERROGATION OF
FOOD CRITIC B.W. BALL

Would you like a cigarette? I'd prefer Talking Mule, 1979 Burgundy. Texture and hue of Bethlehem rust. Notes of must, slate, and pre-coital rouge when tongued to the roof of the mouth. Bold finish, lingering up to seventeen seconds, diminishing to uvular fog. 3.5 stars. *Have they treated you well?* Guard gave me an apple - Brandenburg Barbara. Thick-skinned, sturdy, heavy if held in a non-dominant hand. Loud when bitten, rewarding moisture and zest, firm meat's sweetness haloed by sting. Best served with damp towels. 3 stars. *So what do you remember about last night?* Odor! Van Kuntengraaf goat cheese. Overwhelming to the point of striking a tabletop with one's palm. Once tears dabbed, olfactory reverberations producing surprising amount of saliva and thrill. Fed in 1/4-centimeter tabs, fat, salt, and sour cream dominate at first, the second wave rising with suggestions of chalk, socked feet, and prewar wax. Bordering on gross. Pleasant. 4 stars. *Where were you at 8:30 when the alleged theft of chef Klausmayer's hat occurred?* Table 7, eating a protein snack. Pete's Peanutbutter Pop. Shape of a steamrolled spud on a stick. Color reminiscent of north New Jersey. Looks, tastes, and sounds like silt. Although enjoyable at first, aftertaste distinctly metallic, almost German. Recommended before and after calisthenics. May cause choking. Stick chewable. 2.5 stars. *Your attorney claims you were poisoned by salad dressing. Is that true?* Ali's Valley, Tunisian olive oil. Possibly laced with psychotropic ants. Offered in a carafe instead of an eyedropper. Warning label missing. Stupendous. *Do you recall entering the kitchen area and lunging at chef Klausmayer?* Consumed too many servings before realizing efficacy, resulting in mid-volume howling and Renaissance visions unrecallable upon waking in the borscht scent of the borough's emergency ward. *How are you feeling now, Mr. Ball?* 5 stars. Though I could use some Perrier.

FALLING ASLEEP IN THE YARD

My next breath will be number 382,004,361. I can't yet
see electricity. Nor can I smell magnetic fields, bend
light, grasp underwater intelligence the way an octopus
does, performing her multi-armed fugue, each limb a
melodic line shaping a soul-pleasing whole. Even the
gnats can serenade, lurching past in their galaxy of angst,
droning odes to the unimportance of their tiny faces, the
charity of trees, the curved horizon in the eye of a rat.
A small bird pecks on the windowpane, day in, day out,
unable to cease. Peck-peck. Is it the future visiting its
roots? Peck-peck. Think of all the dusks trapped in
people's clothes. The sleep elevators whose doors part
into halls where things we don't know exist exist. A span
which renders truths we've sensed but deemed invisible
visible.

DEATH AT THE OPERA

Like a brocaded weather balloon the soprano floats across the stage, peacock eyes on her chest. A whiff of opium, the mind ripples, you slump next to your wife in the velvet seat. The air spawns wet pearls, dark blue, plum, pink... You find yourself slicing dates into a white bowl. Apple cut into four green boats, the seeds stunned by light. The knife blade under running water. No sound in the afterlife but the chirr of the insane cricket who fell in through the glare. You pour tea into the cup, look at the wan girl who may be Marie Antoinette. She feeds the two wrens atop the powdered loaf of her hair, spoons soft-boiled egg into your mouth. The cricket trills beneath her hoopskirt, smooth yolk on your tongue. She walks you to an orchard where old men in linen suits point their canes at clouds. Far from the curtain call, from the whisper of your wife, you're no longer the husk of a man in seat seventeen who now appears to have lost count of the times he's circled the sun.

NORTH

Just outside Nome, there lived a well-mannered bear. He went door to door on his hind legs and asked for romance. Most residents declined, but there were a few who invited the bear inside and the night rang with spectacular din. Those days the sun stayed low and the crisp snow held immense paw prints trailing toward the wood. The Nome children would come to church in fur, clutching half-eaten dolls. The congregation spied them from the corners of their eyes. The minister watched from behind the organ and each time he saw a child bite a doll, he played a D minor. The bear in the woods listened. He had a perfect pitch. It hurt to hear the cold organ a quarter note flat, but the bear was too polite to confront the minister. Instead, he covered his ears and whispered of humanity and wildness, snout inches from his favorite fir — a form of incantation. One could almost say it was a prayer.

MIGRATION

A family of five unzips me and climbs inside. I smell burlap and dust as they march up my chest. A wicker trunk dragged by the husband, the wife swerving to the tune of foreign scales. The children point at the sun of my heart, marvel at the pulse of its celadon mouths. Why not, I think to myself, let them spread their checkered cloths on my grass. Let the children pull the levers that lift my arms and tilt my head, dangle from the jungle gym of my ribs. I too had once entered a giant, crouched inside, learned the trade. I grew to dust his skull, the lens of his eye, then became his shell. So why not let these five twitch my fingers, iron my skin, make my prick the tongue of a bell? I can slowly inch away from myself, dwarf from the suit which is now theirs. Look at me slide down the pole, strut away dressed like the emperor.

HORSE AND PUDDLE

I wish I were a short horse standing on a breezy slope somewhere in West Region, Ireland. I'd be the only horse who'd know he is really a human, a wish clad in dark bristles, as if seen by dragonflies. I'd clump to a rain puddle, lower my plush head to the surface, fascinated that while I sit in a wicker chair in California, I can make myself into what I now see in this country water, the brown eyes regarding themselves, lips curled, teeth bared out. In fact, I'd be so fascinated, I'd grow light, begin to drift off, the puddle reflecting less and less of me, until there'd be nothing left, not even the puddle, the hill, or the wind.

THE FRUIT FLIES

It is time to disclose the truth. How they descended on my desk and typed a letter that made very little sense, a logic that matched their size and elusiveness. How I left the study to purchase a cheese sandwich from Herbert, the red-faced grocer, and by the time I returned, there it was, a full-page message placed on the desk, letters pressed into the sheet unevenly, the lines slanted, as running the paper through the typewriter's platen and pressing the keys must have required monumental coordination and strength. I need to write about how they watched me read their text, how they breathed soundlessly on the ceiling, seeing my inverted image, my face like a small pond of lilies and scum. I'm going to write about the time when they typed the first poem for me, how the page was still warm from their fever. They must have labored with the levers of the ancient Underwood, composing verse clusters I couldn't grasp, yet loved. I had collected each subsequent piece and mailed manuscripts - under my name - to the highest floors of the literati castles. Yes, it is time to confess it was they who'd written the books that have brought me prizes. Their unpronounceable names belong on all my work, the committees need to understand it's fruit flies they've liked. I bite into another cheese sandwich, deciphering their new sonnet - magnificently impenetrable, destined for academic frenzy. I feel ready to produce the first draft of my acknowledgement. Once written, I plan to depart the study, allow them to slip out of hidden folds of air, land on the text, scratch on the margins with their tiny pens, mark my modifiers with delicate excrement. When I return, the French doors will be open and in the garden, against the slate of the evening, they will recite to themselves in pulsating formations, the specks of their minds cast like a fine net over the olive tree.

BRAM

The earth of your garden parts and out into the dawn haze in which you slurp your tea, putting off alertness, steps a dwarfish man in brown wool. You rub your jaw and lower yourself onto the three-legged stool he produces from under his coat. Speaking in Walloon, he introduces himself — Bram. He comes from a besieged castle in Liège. Escape tunnels dug by paranoid kings crisscross the country, he tells you, and the one he chose led to your yard. Dry dandelion seeds drift through the halls of your skull, you gaze at your slippers and nod, as if the little man were explaining something you've long known. You retie the belt of your robe, try to recall why it is you understand the language, whether you're an escaped king or a stray serf. But then your soon-to-be-ex appears on the porch and summons you in, ignoring the guest. How rude. The Walloon seems unperturbed. You invite him in for breakfast, but he tips his little hat, plunges head first back into the shaft, the dirt seamlessly closing behind him. A refraction of light? A synaptic glitch you have been no stranger to? You look up, you look sideways, you look down. There is no doubt — you're still sitting on the 12th century milking stool that has no business being in your New Jersey home.

MAN INSIDE AN UNPREPARED PIANO

The composer has inserted his head and upper torso into the lacquered case of the grand piano. Trembling harmonics rise through the symphony hall. Opera glasses aim at his satin braided pants and black swallow-tailed coat writhing under the open wing of the Steinway. He resembles a mechanic under a raised hood of a hearse. To the overseas delegation in the first row he looks more like an obstetrician, or perhaps a lover mining new sounds out of his inamorata. Could it be his teeth plucking the instrument's taut bronze wires? I am the insurance agent in row twenty-seven. In my powder-blue tuxedo I compute for Lloyd's the worth of the man on the stage, gauge the risk to his hands, his mind, the long neck of his wife who hides in the loge behind the glasses and teeth of the music critics. Last week I worked on the case of a jowl-faced bishop who had fallen out of a treehouse. This is so much better. I shift to view the composer's hands as they now squeeze the wooden handles of a large pair of hedge shears. The sounds rising from the piano grow percussive. Sharp pops, snaps, and pulsating bangs, the man almost completely hidden inside the instrument. As the noises crescendo, the lights fade out. The sole illumination left in the hall is the blue glow of my pocket calculator. It is now that the audience hears, for the first time, the composer's voice, a low groan, slowly rising and falling, until his lungs run out of air. When the footlights reignite, he stands in his full height at the front of the stage, unharmed, arms out as if eager to embrace the applauding crowd, dozens of severed piano wires dangling from his fists. Digits flutter through my head like doves, the man in tails holds his pose and veers toward the loge, the strings like an offering of Spanish moss.

CLAUSTRUM AND THE KITCHEN MOUSE

Forget the blue mantle of physics, the bearded men with pipes, the women whose minds burn like jewels. Disregard the scientific dust, the blown glass of so-called life, the arrow of time. You think you know the universe is a long curve that at first glance looks like a straightaway you follow for a few million years, only to arrive dumbfounded and unaged back on your porch. The truth is, there is no curvature to space, no straightness either, all of it humbug. Just remember the long veil at the fringe of waking, weightless, yet self-aware. Recall how in the draft of darkness it undulates, folds and unfolds, thoughts flashing in its lace. *That* is universe. Always keeping you a neuron short of the truth. Are you listening, Cynthia? No - still busy turning the crumb of Gouda in the pink of your paws, convinced my voice is a solar wind, some god's breath blowing from the little heaven of this kitchen.

BARBER'S VISION

There they are again, rounding the corner of Thomas &
Church, the couple with the swan. From my hydraulic
chair they seem noble - the bird on a leash, the husband
in white tux, the wife in nothing. No way to set the watch
by their strolls. On a wet day they'll pass pearled with
dew, all three wrapped in see-through cloaks. How lovely
the clung plastic renders the skin, the breast a whale's eye
inside a wave. The best view after sunset, when traffic
turns their white to pink. Seeing them like this makes me
crave Chinese opera, the three of them entering stage left,
my mallet striking the gong. One of these days I'll burst
after them, ask to be garnished, fitted with wheels. I'll be
your float, I'll say. We'll drift crosstown, let the night
perform its abductions. Next day we'll wake to feed the
swan, fasten the cuff around its neck. In the scent of burnt
pistachios and 5am steam, we'll glide down the boulevard
of breeze-flung trash, our scruffs caught in storefront
mirrors. Across the square, my shop door will be open,
the razor still in the sink, the chairs full of pigeons.

IF I HAD A MAGIC CARPET

—for M.T.

I'd inspect it for mites. Then I'd spend the afternoon asking myself whether I want to fly at all. If so, where? How big would the carpet be? A one-man carpet? A family carpet? Could it fly furniture? Could I reverse-engineer it, mass-produce it, give the street folks higher altitude? I assume it would be steered by the mind, so most likely I'd end up wind-swept and sleepy on your doorstep in Kyoto. Would you ignore the carpet, surprised to see me after twenty-six years, ask me to take off my shoes and come in?

STORY

—for A.L.

There was a woman who lived with an elephant. The elephant adored her. Although the woman felt urges to embrace the elephant, to coo into his immense ears, she never did. It was her way of protecting the dread a heart once broken swaddles itself in, a sensation she loathed, yet was unwilling to shed. To love an idea that only aspires to be real rang safer to her, made her feel pleasantly wistful. She talked to her mugs, spoons, dill sprigs and chairs, but never to the elephant, who just lay in the middle of her room, fashioning large clear tears that collected in a bowl the woman emptied each night into the sink. In a way, it was a content household, and on occasion the elephant hovered a few inches, which was when the woman mopped the linoleum underneath him, trying not to make eye contact. It tickled the elephant, and strangely, it tickled her too. As the woman aged, the elephant grew smaller and smaller, and by the time she was so old she couldn't leave her bed, the elephant was a sugar-cube-sized figurine on her nightstand, a tiny presence she allowed herself to watch from under her covers.

IV

AWE

I waited for it in the fork of a cherry tree. On the LL
train. Made bed for it in my 8th Street room. I left gaps
in sentences where it could land. Dug holes, smoked
ham, lost bets and innocence, granted exculpation
long before it sinned. To track its scent, I stripped
and whorled, committed perfidy, burned effigies and
caramelized figs. I rubbed nougat with licorice and
seven sprigs of dill. I renamed myself after it, just to
see how I rang. Morning, midnight, noon and dusk, I
texted, sexted, called and faxed it. For years and years,
I slept unkept, sculpting pleas and letters of regret.
And then one day it was in my palm. Smooth as a
peanut, smelling of pine. Dzweep, said a jay from the
elm above my head, then bolt-like he dove and
snatched it away.

ERRAND

Stains on the front of my shirt, I've traveled for light years, my senses shut. *Hello, did you find everything you're looking for?* Bound by spiderwork, my top combed into midge clouds, a misconstrued theory of grace. *Thanks for bringing your bags.* Dead, then undead a hundred times, I've seen the torchlit stairwell to the cavern where souls queue up for soup. *Just sign on the pad and press Done.* To grasp impermanence, the unweighable bliss of a leaf in an updraft, its blinks surveying a map the size of the land where you and I are not. *Here's your receipt, you saved $6.27.* Blood? What blood? It's the river of slow light, my barge roped to the willow, my oared arms grained like wood. *Would you like any carryout service today?* Yet by God, there's a charm to your face, as if a wand were tossed into a bottomless gorge, and in its tumble your eyes appeared. *Can I help the next customer?* I see large men with what looks like trumpets, following me into the sundrenched lot. I search for car keys which spacetime, no doubt, has strewn across its void. Here they are, never mind.

ANNE CARSON (SCENE ONE)

We are soundless and airborne. Approaching from the open ocean. We eye the distant coast as a thin slack rope separating the sky from the sea. We speed over the waves toward the land, all but skimming the swell peaks. We don't see our shadow. It may drag behind us or rush ahead, our shape in the water, frictionless, dry. We hear and don't acknowledge the sound of moving air. We feel and don't acknowledge our speed. We smell delight singed by madness. The tang which makes us do what we do. We do not know what it is we do. The shore is getting nearer. We sight dunes and knolls of stirring grass. A group of white huts. Anne reclined on a rock. We slow down. Hover right in front of her face. She looks through us. We can't see who we are. Or what. A ghost of a tern. Japanese wind. Nothing, in its momentary flash of awareness. It is possible that —

DISPATCH FROM FATHER

— J.K. (1921-1986)

Who would have guessed it'd be this smooth?
Everything's the same, I see colors, the bell still
sounds like a bell. The sky full of Holsteins,
hell inches below the underground garage.
Although now I understand the reason for all,
I find myself not caring one way or the other,
recognizing and quickly forgetting, witnessing
and erasing, moving while keeping still. How
nice not to know who I've been! I can read, yet
now language has the shape of an old man
in the crown of the elm. And all of it is love.
No spouses, siblings, parents or offspring, only
ghost molecules in coats and hats, bumping one
another, convinced of their own lives. What's
not to adore about this game, its rules of vapor?
No doors, no mistakes, nothing to explain.
All I do is ripple barley, mist windows, orbit
while you sleep.

POTAGE

Begin with listening. To the crunch of needles under your strides. The tiny birds high in the canopy, flitting from crown to crown. Breathe in, exhale. Do not think.

Each forest has a fallen tree. Deep in the sap-scented quiet, timeworn and grand, it lies on its side. Kneel down. Lay your palms on its bark.

Saw cautiously across the bole, then again, a fraction to the left. What falls off is a slim fragrant disc you'll carry to your cabin.

Smooth and bathe it. Polish the end grain till the tree rings gleam. Drill a hole in the middle and set the disc on the wind-up gramophone. Lean to the horn, let the needle find the grooves.

The tree has an unrushed voice. You won't know what it's saying. Let go. It takes a while to grasp that what you hear is a song. A stately dance. A saraband.

Notice how the branches outside sway, how the evening dims. Let harmonies soak the room. Strike a match to light the lamp. Now, my friend, is the time to cook your soup.

MISPRIZED

It is good to be slow. Walk at leisure, the pace deciding what beauty the mind marks — the subtleties of sameness, the stepped-on black-eyed Susan shaped like the face of a saint with a toothpick in his mouth. I'm always late for the apocalypse. It takes a while to shape up, dress well, to fill the stomach just right for what's coming. When I arrive, what's left smells of hemlock and indignation, the ruins smoldering, a few last figures on fire, fencing with ghosts. The sun is veiled, resembling the moon. By the time I arrive, God is elsewhere, stoned out of his skull, licking icing off a Bundt cake, fingers slick with donut glaze. But oh, the silence. The silence — the one misprized thing about demise. The only thing I can never be late for. The song played after the end, same as the one unheard before the beginning.

WOOD

It was my right leg and Sheryl's left. Turning into wood. Although we didn't have children, she was pregnant by her boss Gus. Her leg was cedar, mine Siberian elm. At first we thought it was the stress from shouting, listening to our voices growing hoarse. But then, as we sat in the divorce lawyer's suite, the spoon I tapped her knee with rang tuning-fork clear. That's when the attorney bent and scrutinized our thighs, scratched diagrams and footnotes I glimpsed over his shoulder — *rare grain, precious, REMOVABLE.* A week later, reconvened at his desk, we learned he'd double his fee. By then my left shoulder and upper arm had wooded and Sheryl feared her fetus had too. The lawyer took off his blazer to wheel us from room to room, the firm's partners viewing our limbs. By June we grew bark. Our bank accounts cleaned, the house liened, we were hauled to the edge of town. Whistling to his shadow, a man labored, now and then pausing to tilt a flask, one hand on the wall where he had us propped. In the late sun we listened. Birdsong, flies, earth scraping the spade.

WAITING ROOM

It's crowded. We're naked and bored. Our skin sticks to the chairs' pink plastic, the muzak marinades the mind. You'd think we'd be grinning, pleased, that some sense of accomplishment, if not ecstasy, would issue from our eyes, yet the prevalent expression here is shellshock. We have no choice but to measure one another, even more so than in our earthly days. There's a fellow hugging a golf club, a woman frowning in her sleep. Beside me, a loose-skinned goon with age spots on his gut, an automatic rifle shielding his crotch. From time to time, an orderly steps in to squeak his orthopedic shoes slowly from one person to the next, saying nothing, poking flesh, jotting notes on his clipboard. We don't know what we're waiting for and are starting to smell. It may be years or hours, all temporal sensation gone. The orderly reappears carrying a wrench. He unfastens a floor hatch we had never noticed, then guides us one by one to the opening, slaps our bare rumps and sends us into the hole, screams fading as we drop back to earth, some spreading umbrellas, others just their arms and legs, the rushing air breaking us up into everything.

ACKNOWLEDGEMENTS

My thanks to the following journals in which these pieces first appeared:

Adroit Journal: "11:37," "Second Date"

Alaska Quarterly Review: "Claustrum and the Kitchen Mouse," "Birds Don't Understand Us"

Bitter Oleander: "Story"

Citron Review: "If I Had a Magic Carpet"

Columbia Poetry Review: "Gamekeeper's Nights"

Copper Nickel: "Caravan"

DIAGRAM: "Falling Asleep in the Yard"

Dunes Review: "Death at the Opera"

Great Ape: "For My Wife's Second Cousin Who Came to Visit for a Week and Still Sleeps in Our Guestroom"

Hawaii Pacific Review: "Man Inside an Unprepared Piano," "Midway"

Hobart: "Bank Job," "On Publishing," "Earl"

jubilat: "Wood"

Little Patuxent Review: "Errand"

Manhattan Review: "Ode to KO," "Nightshift in Produce," "Misprized," "Waiting Room," "F Train," "The Drip"

Massachusetts Review: "God Watching a Sleeping Man," "Police Interrogation of Food Critic B.W. Ball"

Matter: "On Puzzlement"

Michigan Quarterly Review: "Migration"

Mid-American Review: "Fugitive" (2017 Fineline Competition winner)

New Ohio Review: "Awe"

New World Writing: "Foxwhelp," "The Lesson," "The Problem with Truth," "Telegram from the New World," "The World Problem Effect"

Prelude: "Visiting Future In-Laws"

Okay Donkey: "Tchaikovsky"

Phoebe: "Horse and Puddle"

Quarter After Eight: "Tuesday"
RHINO: "The Duck"
Salamander: "The Fruit Flies," "Rumorville," "Transatlantic"
Spillway: "Barber's Vision"
Storm Cellar: "Home Invasion"
Tupelo Quarterly: "Life Insurance (Free Consultation)," "Explaining Marriage to an Alien"
Washington Square Review: "Here"
Wigleaf: "The Last Ferry," "Harmony"
X-R-A-Y: "Hydrogen and Helium"

REPRINTS:

Best Microfiction 2019: "11:37"
FlashFlood: "Gamekeeper's Nights"
FRiGG: "Caravan," "Nightshift in Produce"
X-R-A-Y: "God Watching a Sleeping Man," "Transatlantic," "Tuesday"

I'd like to thank David Rigsbee and Ron Salisbury, whose valuable insights helped with shaping this collection. Many thanks, too, to fellow writers Anna DiMartino, David Gilder, Lloyd Hill, Alison Lanzetta, Michael Mark, Charlie Tatum and Greg White, who read and carefully evaluated many of these poems.

A big thank you to Candice Reffe for selecting this book as the winner of the 2022 Antivenom Poetry Award and for writing such a generous introduction.

I owe much gratitude to Amy Gerstler, Lawrence Raab and Craig Morgan Teicher for their kind words, and to Elixir Press's founder and Editor in Chief, Dana Curtis, for her patience and unyielding vision.

My deep appreciation goes out to Rufina Chen, whose good will, love and friendship has allowed me to maintain a reasonable amount of sanity.

This book is dedicated to my mother.

ABOUT THE AUTHOR

PETER KRUMBACH was born in Brno, Czechoslovakia. After graduating with a degree in visual arts, he left the country, and eventually found his way to the U.S. He worked in commercial art (New York), as a translator and broadcaster (Washington, D.C.), and, for the last 25 years, has lived and written in Southern California.

ELIXIR PRESS TITLES